Everything is Just Great

Everything is Just Great

A STORY OF FAITH, ADVENTURE AND SUCCESS

ROBERT B. PAMPLIN, JR.

MULTNOMAH · PRESS

Portland, Oregon 97266

Cover design by Ted Haines
Cover and interior illustrations by Ted Haines
Edited by Larry R. Libby

EVERYTHING IS JUST GREAT!
© 1985 by Robert B. Pamplin, Jr.
Published by Multnomah Press
Portland, Oregon 97266

Printed in the United States of America

Library of Congress Cataloging in Publication Data

Pamplin, Robert B., 1941-
  Everything is just great.

  1. Pamplin, Robert B., 1941-   . 2. Christian
biography—United States.   I. Title.
BR1725.P23A36   1985   209'.2'4 [B]   85-8788
ISBN 0-88070-118-8

85 86 87 88 89 90 91 – 10 9 8 7 6 5 4 3 2 1

To my family.

CONTENTS

INTRODUCTION

I have been accused of playing the "glad game." This was a game created by Eleanor Porter, for her heroine, Pollyanna.

Pollyanna tried to find good in everything. One year, at Christmas, she asked for a doll. When the presents got mixed up and she was given a pair of crutches, she didn't complain. Instead, she said, "Isn't it great that I don't have a broken leg and don't have to use these?"

Now I will admit to one of Pollyanna's dominant emotions—an irrepressible, enthusiastic belief that everything that happens in my life will be for the best. Am I guilty, then, of a rationalization inherent in the glad game? Not really. For my emotion is based on reality, not simple semantics or some shallow mind game. It is founded on the belief that the drama of physical pain and suffering, the anxiety of death, and the excitement of success have been laid out in a grand design—a master plan that is in God's hands.

The plan itself grows out of a relationship with God—and the overpowering conviction that He has purpose for my life.

CHAPTER

1

E. C. was the greatest fisherman on earth.

That, at least, was my firm conviction when my Dad first took me fishing in the swamps of the Savannah River, in eastern Georgia.

E. C. didn't have to use a lot of the tricks other fishermen did to catch jack, his specialty. He didn't have to spit on the bait, or hold his mouth right, or even wear a special fishing hat—although all that helped, he used to tell me with a wink.

E. C. just used an old, bent cane pole, with a string and a cork bob tied on it, and a hook baited with worms. But he could catch more jack than all the others put together. At least, to hear him tell it that was the case.

I was six years old when Dad introduced me to the swamp. While there—usually on a weekend—we shared a one-room shack with river rats that had to be chased out of the pot-bellied stove before E. C. or one of the other men could cook a pot of squirrel or catfish stew.

Since the shack was small, cooking odors of a good stew would fill the room with an aroma that tantalized

TED HAINES

already eager appetites. When the meal was finally ready, we would dig in like hogs—and probably sounded like them, too.

After the bones had been sucked clean and the last drop of stew soaked up by hot biscuits, we would all sit back and listen to stories of fishing and hunting.

E. C., of course, would usually start off, often with a "try to match this" challenge. Tilting back in his chair, the light from the kerosene lamp dancing on his face, he would begin with a line like this:

"The Savannah River bobwhite are the smartest quail in the world." Waiting to make sure he had secured our full attention—sometimes a good twenty seconds or more—he would go on with his story.

"Those bobwhite'll either get up behind you when you think they are in front, or they'll get a tree between them and you—just when you shoot. They caused me to shoot more trees! Lemme tell you, I can remember one time when I finally got a shot at one. I hit that darn bird—killed him dead—but you know what he did? He grabbed a leaf and, like a blanket, covered himself up on the way down so I couldn't find him. Now, that is one smart bird."

Finally, after all had had their chance at topping E. C., we would arrange our blankets on the floor for the night. Then, when the lamps were extinguished, the real action would begin. It was as if you had given all the rats in the swamp the starter's flag, because they came out in force. The roof of the shack was made of tin, and their running up and down sounded like a bowling alley on Saturday night. The older men had experienced these giant-size rats all of their lives, but to a young boy, peering into their eyes at floor level made me shrink up closer to Dad. Soon, however, the exhaustion of a long day would conquer my fear and I wouldn't know a thing until someone was boiling a pot of coffee next morning.

A young boy learns respect for the swamp in a hurry, which was part of the reason Dad took me there. I don't recall being afraid—my feelings were more fascination for the cone-shaped cypress knees protruding out of the murky water, the quicksand, and wildlife. Gators, rattlers, and water moccasins were native to the region, and I quickly learned proper regard for each.

Those were great days, with freedom to experience what early natives must have acclaimed as the majesty of adventure and excitement. With varied animal life, thick woods and vines challenging each step, and the clean yet heavy smell of a still marsh, these Georgia backwoods were exhilarating. There was a sense of daring and mystery that could keep you in a state of wonder all day long. Memories include ducks stirring to sudden flight as a small boat encroached silently into their domain . . . the deep-throated bellows of hound dogs on the trail of a deer . . . the incessant chatter of the wily gray squirrel, which brought many a good meal of barbecue or brunswick stew.

As Dad and I went back time and again, I also learned to respect the collection of individuals who were our companions in the cabin. Besides E. C. the fisherman, there were loggers, mill workers, and moonshiners. They were all friends of my father, who was an executive with Georgia Hardwood Lumber Company (now Georgia-Pacific Corporation), then a small but burgeoning lumber company. Even as a youngster I quickly realized that true equality reigned at a hunting and fishing camp. Being a corporate bigwig did not place one on a higher plane than a timber faller in that clapboard cabin. A man was measured by the number of fish he could catch or birds he could shoot—not his title. That's a lesson I never forgot.

While the social lessons of swamp living may have been subtle, the majority of my training as a young

southern gentleman was anything but subtle. The lessons were driven home with compelling emphasis. The first words I learned to say after "Mama" and "Daddy" were "Yessir" and "Yes'm," and if I didn't use these designations while talking to my elders, I could expect a swift—and painful—reminder.

A child in the South jumps through many hoops which are intended to give a young person a solid foundation for determining right from wrong. Part of it is church training, beginning with Sunday school at a very early age, but it includes the strict discipline imposed by one's elders: parents, grandparents—and often loving servants.

My mother was the family disciplinarian, the one charged with "bringing me up," and the one from whom I received the most correction when I did something wrong. She was swift, fair, and unswerving in her application of child justice—often with a switch—and thus played the role of first sergeant in my early life. Dad, on the other hand, being of a somewhat stern nature, did not have to act quite so much the disciplinarian. I respected the authority implicit in his being.

As I look back, I realize that instilling values was a significant aspect of the relationship I had with my parents. Survival skills, the work ethic, respect for one's elders, right and wrong, and a strong faith in God were all part of what was being imparted.

Still . . . it is exceedingly difficult to appreciate the instillation of lifetime values when you've been sent out to cut a switch that will be applied to YOUR behind because you did something wrong. I had to choose just the right kind of switch, too. It had to be thick enough not to break when used, because if it broke too quickly I would be sent out to cut another one and the punishment would start all over. Switch selection became something of a science.

There are two things
that can never be
taken away from you:
education and a
belief in God. For,
once you have them,
they are with you
always.

As I reflect on those formative years, I realize that much of the correction wasn't because I was a "bad" kid, but was due to my being part of a particular environment—and having elders who insisted on clarity between right and wrong.

During my preschool years I lived in an apartment complex in Augusta, Georgia. My playmates were a rough-and-tumble bunch, and a pecking order was quickly established. From my youngest days I had been taught to stick up for what I believed, and that often led to fights.

Actually, getting a fight started with that group of kids didn't take much effort at all. It seems like we were always fighting over something. I was small for my age, and some of the other kids tried to take advantage of that. But I never did back off—and got a good share of lickings because of it. It evened out, because I gave out some good ones, too.

One of those fights made my mother angrier than I had ever seen her. I had had an accident at school—practically tearing off my ear on a barb-wire fence. A doctor had done a good job of stitchery, then had wrapped a bandage around and around my head, almost turban style. The doctor, who knew the nature of kids in that area, admonished me not to get in any fights and mess up his careful work.

When I went outside to play, Mother also was precise in her instructions: "Bobby, don't you dare get in a fight, or you'll get a real whipping when you get in!"

I don't recall now what triggered it, but less than five minutes after I got outside, I was down on the ground and one of the bigger kids in the neighborhood was pounding on my head, blow after blow. By the time I got away, the bandage was soaked with blood, and Mother had real reason to see red. Fortunately, the damage to the ear was superficial, and the doctor was able to sew it up again as good as new. He had a few choice words for me, though, and Mother too was true to her word.

I don't think that kids fight as much today as we did then. I doubt that it's because we are any more civilized now; more likely it is because youngsters today have more organized activities and other distractions.

For the kids in small southern communities, especially those thrown together in somewhat crowded living conditions, fighting was at least second nature, if not first.

That, too, is part of a Southern heritage. It is no accident that the War Between the States went on long after the Southern forces had every reason to stop; manpower, food, ammunition, and even real estate were severely restricted. But the will to continue fighting died a hard death—if it ever died at all.

Most Southern children learn about the Civil War at an early age, either in school or through family discussions. The Rebel Yell, "Dixie," and even awareness of the Stars and Bars most likely came before national traditions to a young Georgian in the 1940s, even though the country was engulfed in another war. There really are those in the South who have never accepted Lee's surrender. It is difficult to explain to a Northerner the intensity of feelings—the bitterness—that remains ingrained in the Southerner's fiber even after the passage of more than a century since the war was fought.

My own indoctrination to the Civil War came in a most graphic way. We would often spend summers and vacations at the old Virginia farm where my father was reared. The property was near Petersburg, site of many battles and a long siege. The land still yielded artifacts from the war when Dad was a youth—and even when I visited there years later. Dad used to tell about finding lead mini-balls which he and his chums would cut up to

make sinkers when they went fishing. A breastwork on the property was a battle line, something my father saw every day when he was a child.

Keeping the memories of those battles alive was a sacred trust for my grandmother. She constantly related tales of the war that had been told to her by her parents and grandparents.

"Bobby," Grandmother would say, "much of the Battle of Petersburg was fought on this farm. Your people *lived* the War Between the States—it was their back yard, so what I tell you about your legacy as a Southerner is the truth! I know. I was there! And Bobby . . . don't let anyone tell you different."

My grandmother was a feisty lady. She knew what was right, and didn't give an inch. She could tell stories that practically let me smell the acrid burning of gunpowder or hear the cries of injured soldiers. Her family had lost kinfolk and they had lost land. The family status slipped from that of landed gentry to genteel poverty in the intervening years. Perhaps the only constant was pride.

Grandmother had a firm chin, and she held her head high, even though you could see in her eyes the pain and humiliation that the Civil War and ensuing years had etched in her heart. Fueled by her stories, my imagination coursed wildly when I played "war" on the farm. I could visualize men of the Virginia Confederacy huddled in pocket caves against sporadic rifle fire and cannon blast, awaiting orders for the next charge. I could even imagine their conversations as they had a brief respite from the terrors of battle. These were Southern boys: They would talk about the barbeques, complete with all the succulent foods the likes of which they hadn't seen for years. They would talk about their sweethearts and other girls they knew from the grand balls or the promenades through Richmond . . . beautiful ladies with thin waists accentuated by an active bustle. They would talk of horses racing across lush meadows, and warm summer nights and fireflies and honeysuckle. But all too soon the soft, low chatter of homesick boys would end in a choke of rage and fear—and the green Virginia countryside would erupt in flame and horror and death and the sun would be hidden in the smoke of battle.

Inevitably, Grandmother told me, the conversations of those brave soldiers would swing around to the "whys" of war: Why the destruction . . . the pillage . . . the carnage . . . the futility? The answers always would be the same: It was not that the Southerner approved slavery, the bondage of another man. After all, the system was reconciling itself with its non-economic failings, and would have washed itself clean in time. But the South would not be subjected to the dictatorial rule of the North. The South would have freed the slaves if justly compensated, for the chief asset of the agrarian South was attached to this human ownership . . . that asset plus the principles of life that shaped the Southern gentleman: genteel expressions of caring, understanding, a conservative manner, and an unswerving belief in God.

These were the kinds of stories with which my grandmother filled my head on each visit to the farm. She accepted—as did my parents—the duty of steeping me in the cultural heritage of the South.

My grandfather, John Pamplin, had been born in 1861, the year the Civil War began. I did not know him, for he died before I visited the farm, and Grandmother had remarried. The family cultivated thirty acres of the two-hundred-acre farm with mule and plow. The farm was the sole source of support for my grandparents and their three sons. It was a hard life, but they didn't think of themselves as poor.

A man's character
is the most
important asset
he has.

They raised a few cows for milk and cream, chickens and hogs, with the hogs being the main meat staple for the family. Although the farm had electricity, it had no running water, relegating certain necessities of life to an outhouse complete with a mail-order catalog for reading and other duties.

Grandmother cooked on a wood stove, and one of the chores of the boys was to see that the wood box was stocked. I got my share of chopping and splitting when I visited there, too. All water for use in the house was carried in from the well.

Getting the pail to the house with water still in it could be a major problem, too. Big people could carry two pails at a time, and thus be balanced, but a youngster had all he could do to carry one in front of him with both hands—making the journey from the well one of bumps, trips, sloshes, and spills.

Crops raised on the farm were taken to town each Saturday and were sold out of the back of an old truck. That provided some cash for staples that were not raised, such as salt and sugar, plus clothes, feed, and other needs.

Pork was still the primary meat source on the farm when I visited as a boy. My grandmother did have a refrigerator, but even so, some of the pork she kept in it aged well beyond the time when it should have been used for human consumption. I didn't know what was wrong with it: I just knew it smelled bad and tasted funny, but that you ate what you could get when you were at the farm.

Grandmother sold fryer chickens as well as eggs, and the ritual for slaughtering the chickens was one of fascination to me as a child—despite the fact that it was gory. As any farm kid knows, the saying "running around like a chicken with its head cut off" has basis in fact, as do many other clichés. Decapitated chickens can—and

do—run around in a wild frenzy. Grandmother Pamplin solved that indelicacy, however, by tying the birds' feet to a clothesline, so that they would hang head down. Then she methodically cut off their heads with a large knife, cautioning me to stay clear of the spurting blood.

It wasn't a pretty sight, yet I don't remember it with anguish or disgust—merely as a natural step that a farmer took to provide food on the table.

Often when evening shadows crawled across the porch of the old farm house, Grandmother, quiet and motionless, would sit looking out over the freshly plowed sandy soil. Her weathered countenance held no mysteries, for the farm itself was a show-place of history. The ancient house was deteriorating in the weather, and the outhouse leaned to the wind. Chickens roamed freely through the yard, leaving their droppings at will. Since I never wore shoes during the summer, I was constantly scraping my feet on the grass, especially before I was allowed into the house.

The farm was fun for me as a youngster, but to the adults who depended on it for their food and shelter—their very existence—stubbornness, hard work, and a good measure of faith gauged their mettle.

Grandmother was a peaceful lady except when her dander was up. Under such circumstances you ran for cover; she had that unbending "stare the man down" look, and woe to the person who would cross words with her during such a spell. I remember distinctly one occasion when I turned the churn over and caused a terrible mess, what with sour milk and butter filling the cracks between the floor boards. She would have whaled me good if my father had not spanked me first.

There were other times when she would sound all fired up, but her tone only reflected the combative, stubborn characteristics of a Virginian. That happened most frequently during family discussions about almost anything, from what the President had said to how to treat a neighbor's sick cow. When opinions differed, defense of a position would carry with it the force of a searing red-hot iron; the so-called discussions would get quite heated. I came to realize that a Virginian is a very opinionated individual.

Grandmother's opinions carried a lot of weight, not just because they were practical, but because they were usually right. She was most sure of herself when telling me about the South, the real South.

"It's a good land, Bobby. It's raised your father and his father, and other men like them. Whatever a man does, wherever he goes, when he has grown up here, he'll always carry the rub of the Southern landscape. He can wash it off his face, but he won't flush it out of his soul. It doesn't matter if he lives in a tar-paper shack or a mansion—or wears bibbed Roebucks or a coat and tie. He'll be what he is—a Southern gentleman."

As Grandmother was a very determined lady, she wanted her sons to have opportunities that she and Grandfather had not had. The phrase "upward mobility" may not have been coined in the South, but it was a time-honored tradition that dated back to the antebellum years when a true plantation and subsequent wealth in land and slaves was the dream of many a settler on the virgin soils.

Grandfather had gone to school three days of his life, had not found it to his liking, and had never gone back. Yet despite the meager farm income that the family had, all three Pamplin sons graduated from college, seeking education as the first step toward a better way of life. But the tradition of hard work on the farm was not lost in the process. Somewhere in the Pamplin genes, a hereditary trait of achievement was established.

Though I was not conscious of such a trait in those early days on the family farm, or at the apartment house

Do what you think
is right, then forget
about it.

where we lived, I was intensely aware that pleasing my father was a goal at which I had to succeed.

Many young men today—even in grade school—have a chance to make a dad proud through organized athletics, but in our neighborhood we did not have such an opportunity. Sand-lot and pick-up games were the extent of team sports, and rarely did any father come out to watch one of those melees.

But in my case, I had another chance to win my father's approval—through hunting. To most Americans, baseball is the national sport. Not to the Southern male. Hunting is not only the number-one pastime, it is a way of life. My journey along that path began when Dad gave me my first BB gun at age five. That act signed the death warrant for many of the birds in our neighborhood. Big folks hunted birds; I hunted birds. What I didn't know then is that there are such things as seasons and limits, and that some birds are game birds, and others are not to be hunted.

When I began hunting in earnest with the men of the swamp, my job was to help clean the game the men had killed. From the very beginning my instincts told me that if I did a good job and made Dad proud of me, he would look good in the eyes of his companions. Approval of my father was important to me, and I strived hard to make him look like the best dad in the world. He would inspect my work with a critical eye, expecting a professional job before I could participate in shooting the game.

My first "real" hunting was for squirrels, a popular staple in our meat diet at that time. The swamp was heavily populated with squirrels, and after giving me lessons in how to shoot them, Dad stationed me in an area where there were many nests and hickory nut cuttings. He pretty much left me on my own while he covered another location. Dad would put gunnysacks on the

TED HAINES

Make sure it is your
own work and you
have done your best.
No one can ask for
more.

ground for me to sit on, to help keep off chiggers and other crawly critters. I was under strict orders not to leave my stand, and by then I'd heard enough stories about the snakes and quicksand that I didn't question that authority.

I quickly learned that the hunter didn't have to hunt squirrels—it was the other way around. Stalking a squirrel is largely a useless activity. The little creatures will always keep the tree between themselves and the hunter. Chattering and scolding, they will move around the tree just ahead of you—making it all but impossible to take aim. But the stationary hunter can silently wait them out, and often get clear shots. A squirrel's curiosity will always overcome his fear. Minutes after the gun report that fells one of their fellows, others will be out nosing about in the branches. It wasn't unusual for Dad and me to sit at our stations and kill dozens of squirrels in an outing.

Those hunting days represented some of the best quality of time I had to spend with my father when I was young, for he was working long hours at Georgia Hardwood and had little time during the week to share with me. Some of the time he did spend at home, though, was unique. I doubt that there are many fathers who read annual reports or Wall Street Journal articles to their children for bedtime stories, but that's what I grew up with. Dad was making sure I received a proper business education. It was an influence that I treasure— it not only developed a special relationship between my father and me, but has also had a substantial effect on my life in the business world.

It's good that I was getting that business education from my father, because I was getting little education of any kind from the public schools in Augusta at the time. Born in 1941, I represented the leading edge of the "baby boom." My first-grade class was held in an auditorium where we sat in chairs rather than at desks. We had to try to balance boards on our laps for writing surfaces, an exercise that probably was more useful later for buffet dinners and church socials than it was for learning in school. Grading at that time consisted of "S" and "U"—satisfactory or unsatisfactory, and I always seemed to get "S." I did particularly well with math and memory work, but my reading and English skills were poor. Over all, I remember those early school days as being happy times—but not having much to do with learning.

The opposite is true of my early church experience. When one is reared in a particular environment, he always carries certain aspects of that environment. I was reared in a Christian church and indoctrinated with Bible stories. Sunday was church day, beginning with Sunday school, then the morning church service, and back again at night for another service. I was allowed to play some between Sunday school and the service, since Dad was an usher. But when it came time for the sermon, I was expected to be at my seat beside my mother.

Like my father, my mother had a profound effect on how my life would unfold. Under her realm of responsibility fell the day-to-day discipline and creating of a Christian environment. Each morning we would gather at the breakfast table for a devotional. And since my mother was a Sunday school teacher, the material was usually a serial view of what was to happen Sunday. She had a way of casting the biblical characters in the drama of their culture, making the story real as if it were being paraded in front of you. Of course, the visual aids of scenery and people, which she spent hours making, increased the realism. We had our own stage and dramatic production each Sunday. I must place squarely on her shoulders a generous portion of credit for sealing me as one of Christ's own.

My most memorable church experience came when I was seven or eight years old. Billy Graham came to Augusta. The Rev. Mr. Graham was just getting started at that time, and he stayed at our minister's house while he was in town. I heard him speak, and his zeal and enthusiasm for Christ were like nothing I had ever heard before. At Mr. Graham's invitation, I truly accepted Jesus Christ into my life.

Little did I know what a profound influence that acceptance would have on the rest of my life.

CHAPTER
2

Though Billy Graham had given me a new window into my Christian beliefs, it wasn't until years later that I began to see through it clearly.

In fact, it may not have been until after Dad moved the family to the Northwest, when Georgia-Pacific began expanding its holdings, that I could see ways in which Christ's teachings had meaning in my life. It was then that I began to come to grips with a life-shaping paradox of faith: that good could come from adversity.

I had always been a healthy, active child, so my parents were not at all sure what was wrong with me when I suddenly began losing weight—and energy—shortly after entering the sixth grade.

They took me to a doctor, and I can remember that visit as if it were yesterday: the time of day, the sunny weather, and most of all the stark, white walls of his plain office. The physician took one look at me and said:

"You've got hepatitis."

He could tell from the yellow cast of my skin and of my eyeballs. As it turned out, his diagnosis from that

A disappointment should only be temporary. Character is not built by accepting defeat, but by snatching success from the jaws of defeat. Plan how to overcome the setback and move ahead with confidence.

external observation was accurate, but to make matters worse I also had a viral infection—and intestinal flu.

The next few months were about as miserable as a kid can endure. I was forced to spend most of my time at home and in bed, and had to have a tutor to attempt to keep up with school studies. I had very little energy, and was so worried about my health that I began to think of myself as being a weakling.

This sedentary life was very different and difficult for me. I had always been very active and loved sports of all kinds, although a trick knee had been somewhat limiting since grade school. I had learned of the knee problem very suddenly one day: one moment I was running down field at full speed with a football, then after making a cut, I was on the ground, writhing with pain. It was almost as if I had been blind-sided, except the injury came from within. The knee felt deformed as the cap was twisted to the side of the joint.

I was hauled to the doctor, who unceremoniously reached his hand up my pant leg and twisted the kneecap back in place. He then put the leg in a cast, but that was the beginning of a long, uncomfortable experience with the trick knee. It plagued me through high school freshman basketball until the day of reckoning came—I had an operation to move the kneecap down so it would not ride so high. My leg never fully recovered from that operation. And as a result I was limited in the type of athletic activities in which I could participate. But things have a way of working out.

A very simple movie that was capturing the hearts of the viewing public at that time was "Wee Gordie." It was about a Scotsman who was determined to make his weak body into a showcase of muscle and strength. He left the windows wide open at night to let the brisk Scottish night air infuse him with its vigorous qualities. He started a weight program, and through hard work developed himself to become a contender for the gold medal in the Olympics. What inspiration! And for me, the timing was perfect.

The story of "Wee Gordie" somewhat paralleled one that I had read about on the backs of comic books when I was ill with hepatitis: that of Charles Atlas, the body-builder who had transformed himself from a ninety-seven-pound weakling to a mighty specimen of strength and vigor.

The knee operation had caused permanent weakness in my leg, and my over-all physical condition was not to my liking at the time. But if Atlas and Gordie could change themselves, so could I! Sending away for the Charles Atlas Program is not something a kid tells his peers about. Nevertheless, I became a subscriber to the Atlas program, and after a while I could see results!

It was a fairly simple regimen: push-ups, sit-ups, chin-ups, and other good, old-fashioned exercises combined with weight-lifting. It also taught a way of life: development of pride in your physical being by exercising and eating properly.

The Atlas program did something else for me that was exceedingly important. It led me to Joe Loprinzi, trainer at Portland's Multnomah Athletic Club and a devotee of weight lifting.

Joe is a man for whom fitness was a way of life, and he approached it with a fervor that was infectious. My immediate goal was to overcome the atrophy in my injured leg. But working with Joe quickly showed me that the weights I had started lifting in the Atlas program could be pushed to new heights under the supervision of this master lifter.

At first Joe's regimen called for me to be at the club each Tuesday and Thursday, but as my muscles began to show noticeable improvement, I found myself adding days.

I would probably have been content with basic body-building, except for what happened one day in the early fall. The football team's practice had been called off and many of the members were in the weight room trying to build strength for the season ahead. Being a competitive lot, they began to challenge each other as to how much they could military press. (That is bringing the bar bell to your chest and pushing it overhead without jerking your body or bending your knees.) Of course I got into the contest, and with all the cheering and laughter, Joe's attention was diverted in our direction. Now, these players were husky, weighing one-hundred-eighty to two-hundred pounds. I weighed a hundred twenty-five pounds at the time.

The contest started at seventy-five pounds and moved upward rapidly. Surprising to me, I was keeping up. Finally at a hundred-thirty pounds, I had reached my limit. The football players went further, but after they had all left, Joe pulled me aside.

"Bob, how much did you lift?"

"One-hundred-thirty pounds," I said.

"That is very exceptional for your weight, Bob. Do you realize that only about five percent of the people in the world can lift their body weight?"

In the same breath he said, "I believe that you could become a weight lifter."

"A weight lifter?"

"Bob, there are three Olympic lifts—those that are used in the Olympics—and there are AAU sponsored meets throughout the United States. I believe that with some training you could make the Club team and do well in these meets. There really aren't a lot of people who have natural strength and can lift their weight. You have that gift. Think about it and we will talk later."

Well, we did talk later, and I did begin to train as a lifter. The regimen was tough, splits for the clean and jerk, dead lifting for the clean, pressing off a rack for the press . . . But after months of this regimen and Joe's careful coaching, he was ready to enter me into the Oregon State Championships.

"This Saturday is the meet," Joe said. "You will travel down to Eugene with me. I don't want you to lift two days before the meet so your muscles will have a chance to rest. Eat only fruits, vegetables, and lean meat. No Coke, desserts, sweets, and stay away from the starches. Your weight is borderline at 123 pounds. When you weigh in we don't want you to have to sweat it off. You will lose too much strength. And Bob, get plenty of rest." Such lectures had been going on for several months now.

Saturday finally arrived. That morning early I weighed in at the Club to make sure that my weight was okay. It was, and we were off to Eugene, which is about a hundred and ten miles from Portland. On the way down, Joe was prepping me with last-minute instructions.

"Don't bend your back on the press, Bob, and keep your knees locked. Once you get the weight up, lock your elbows and don't drop the weight until the judge claps—you have to hold it two seconds. Whatever you do, don't start with too much weight. You have three chances at each lift, so don't get yourself in a position where you cannot make a lift. It will destroy your total."

The time passed quickly. I had weighed in, chalked my hands, and had a swig of fresh orange juice and honey to supercharge the adrenalin.

"Pamplin," I heard over the P.A. system. My name was called for the second lift in the press. I shot off the bench like a rocket and as quickly blurted out "one-hundred-forty-five pounds," the weight I intended to try. The attendants arranged the appropriate weight on the bar and then I was over it concentrating on all the techniques which Joe had patiently taught me for months. Hands equal distance from the center, arms straight

A treed squirrel only has one way to go. Don't close any door because of pride; keep your options open.

down from the shoulders. Back straight, knees bent. Pull up quickly and flip the wrist so that the bar will fall on the chest as you come to a standing position. Lock the knees, push the bar over your head, lock the elbows, hold for two seconds, listen for the clap. It went so smoothly, my mind was still going over the details as I was dropping the weight at the end of the lift.

As I returned to the bench, Joe greeted me with a grin that told me I had done all right. He had a paper in front of him and pushed it in front of my face. "Bob," he exulted, "you have just broken the state record!"

I looked at him with a vacant stare. In my mind I was asking, what does that mean? He had to say it a second time before I fully realized what he had said. I was so excited—I knew that at my last chance at the press I would push that bar through the ceiling. And I did lift a greater weight than I ever had before.

But there are also those humbling things in life.

It so happened that I held the state record for only fifteen minutes . . . because another competitor lifted a greater amount than I had. But I will always remember that I was a state record holder, even if it was for only a few minutes. Surprisingly, Joe has never forgotten either. I saw him recently on the street when I was with my youngest daughter. After I introduced her, my old coach began to telling her about my "state weight-lifting record." I didn't even feel too bad when he mentioned that it was only for those few minutes.

Competitive weight lifting is not an easy task, especially for a growing boy. One thinks of weight lifters as the bulky, muscular two-hundred-fifty-pounders who constantly eat spaghetti to keep up their bulk. That may be true for the heavy weights, but for me it was just the opposite. My best weight for competition was the one-hundred-twenty-three pound class, and to hold that weight I was on a constant diet through high school.

Every morning I had wheat germ oil and vitamins, and a month before a meet I had to carefully watch what I ate, usually sticking to just lean meat and vegetables at night. Two days prior to the competition, I would try not to drink any water, and the day of the meet, before weigh in, I'd go to the steam room to try to shed any extra pounds that might put me in the next higher class.

The difference in my personal weight could be costly, as I found at a northwest regional championship. I just wasn't able to starve or sweat off the final three pounds, and had to go into the one-hundred-thirty-two pound class rather than the one-hundred-twenty-three. As it turned out, in all categories—Clean and Jerk, Snatch, and Military Press—I lifted as much as I ever had, and took third in that higher class. It would have been an easy win in my normal category.

As an adult, I have few regrets about my childhood and youth, but one choice I might make differently does involve weight lifting. Because of my placing second in the Pacific Coast championships, I was invited to participate in the Junior Nationals, held that particular year in California. I decided not to enter, partly because I was concerned that I might not earn one of the three places in my weight category, but mainly because I had a girl friend who wanted to go to the big dance at school. Ah, priorities! As it turned out, had I lifted my usual amount, I would have placed second in the meet, based on the scores that were published after the championship. Who knows, I might have won first if I had pressed the leader.

That happened to me once in a meet. The guy in the lead had me beat cold, but he got cocky and tried too much weight on the Clean and Jerk—and couldn't handle it. I won the meet, and I also profited from his mistake. From that time on I was careful not to attempt a lift I wasn't confident I could handle.

While the regimen of weight lifting was hard, most

My father's father told him, and my father told me, "I would rather follow you to the grave than have you become an alcoholic."

of the rest of my time in high school was not. My best buddies were a bunch that enjoyed a good time, but my friends in school were not limited to any one group. I can't help feeling that reflects back to the early days in the apartment and at the swamp, where I was comfortable with all kinds of people. In high school it was particularly important at election time: I seemed to be able to pull together a coalition for class elections, and held several positions as a result, including senior class president.

With those positions came responsibilities. Some of those I handled well—with a couple of notable exceptions. It was one of the latter instances which nearly ended my high school career—prematurely.

A friend, Dick, and I were planning a pledge party for the Deacons, a social club of which I was president. We had lined up the cream of the freshman boys to attend, and it was important to give them a good time. As I recall, Dick was suggesting we have a dance, though he said:

"Most of the members think we should have a beer party. They seem to think it would be cool to show the freshmen how the big boys do things. Problem is, we don't have a place. None of the members' parents will be away Saturday. I guess the decision is up to you," Dick concluded.

"I don't know," I said. "A pledge party is a school function, and if we get caught with beer, we'll really be hung out to dry."

"But we've got to impress those pledges," returned Dick. "It's our great opportunity." "Okay, let's do it, but you will have to find the place," I said. "I'll post on the activities board that we are going to have a pony ride this Saturday." (A pony ride meant that we were going to have a party with a pony keg. Such terminology was used to keep the principal in the dark.) "See you this Saturday.

I've got to get to class—there's the bell."

That is how the now infamous keg party and my suspension from high school began. My last year in high school was to be the grandest of times. I had moved through all the hurdles of being an underclassman and now I was looking forward to taking advantage of senior status. I was even ready to take a few chances, knowing that some of the escapades we had planned were border-line delinquent.

This, mind you, was the glorious 1950s—the time of Be Bop Be Loula, rock, the hop, and Elvis. At school we had quite a mix in the student body. We had the greasers sporting the duckbutt hair style, black leather jackets, white tee shirts with cigarettes rolled up in the short sleeve, and tight blue jeans that tapered at the ankle. The tough guys. The more knife marks across the stomach, the greater the respect. In particular, one giant who occasionally attended P.E. was covered with knife scars. I remember the conversations that centered on him that first day of school.

"Did you see those scars when he dressed down for P.E.?" We all concluded that he was really tough—and he had to be mean, too. He was tough all right, but later we found that he was not mean at all. He just lived in a rough neighborhood.

Some kids were the students, some with horn-rimmed glasses, or four eyes, as we would call them; others with soft skin and a little baby fat cushion around the middle. Another group were the floaters, young people just putting in their time, and not really par-ticipating—whether by their own choice or because of not being accepted.

Finally, there were the "popular kids," the jocks, the class officers, the members of social clubs, and those with labels, such as "best dressed," "most likely to suc-ceed," "cutest couple," "most handsome," and so on.

Usually you didn't just fall into a group; you had to earn your position. For instance, to be a real greaser it took either a souped-up motorcycle or a mass of knife scars. And a recipient would wear such marks with pride, like a German duelist with a scar across the cheek.

So, after three years, I felt I had arrived. It was my intention to make the Deacons the best club. And there was no better way to entice the impressionable freshmen to become members than to show them how worldly we were. That's why we planned that keg party.

We decided to deliver the keg in a hearse. After all, who would imagine that a group of teenage boys would be carrying around a keg of beer in a hearse? Everything was set. The keg was secured, the hearse gassed, and the prospective members invited.

We held the party under a viaduct. Woods were on each side and the traffic noise would certainly hide any laughter and shouting. We were well into the swing of things when a resident of the neighborhood came strolling down the trail. "Oh no," I exclaimed. No sooner had I gotten out the words than Dick yelled "Run!" Dick and I grabbed the keg and ran up the bank to the waiting hearse. I stomped on the gas and we both thought we had made a good get-away.

But the next Monday, in my third period class, I received a summons from the vice-principal. He requested my presence in his office—immediately. As I walked in the door I could tell trouble was at an advanced stage. Dick and some of the other Deacons were sitting around the vice principal's desk, and they all had very long faces.

"Come in and sit down," said the vice-principal. His voice was matter-of-fact, but carried a distinct edge to it. And he didn't beat around the bush, either. "Did you and Dick organize a beer party for new pledges last Saturday?"

I was speechless.

"Well?" he said. I remained silent, not knowing what to say. He didn't wait long for my answer. He spun around in his chair and picked up two quart jars that were sitting on his credenza. "These were brought in by someone strolling down by the viaduct on Macadam. They were used by boys having a beer party there." The tone of voice was getting rather sharp now. This was big trouble.

"Is that right?" I said, fervently hoping he would not throw those three piercing words at me again. My hopes went for naught.

"*Was it you*?" he demanded.

My balloon was pricked immediately, because he said: "It was you and all these boys present. We know it."

My fear was beginning to subside somewhat, and as bravely as I could, I challenged him as to how he could be certain that it was us. Was that ever a mistake. He dismissed the others and then he let me have it. "Bob, I have lost all my patience," he said with a shrill. If I had not been in such trouble I might have laughed at his high-pitched voice. Then he spelled it out very clearly.

"You have two options, and just two. Normally I would expel you, but since you have good grades and have not been in trouble before, I will only suspend you if you make a complete confession right now."

My thoughts ran the gamut. "I can't rat on the others, but, boy, am I in a pile of trouble."

"Can I think it over during the lunch hour?" I asked with all the courage I could muster.

"Get out and come back at one o'clock," he semi-yelled. As soon as I left his office, I made a beeline to the cafeteria. I found Dick and explained the situation. Then I asked, "What did you tell him?"

"We told him the whole story," he said. "Our backs were to the wall. We had no other option."

At one o'clock sharp I was waiting at the vice-principal's door. My confession was short and simple: "We had a beer party and I was a part of the group."

His reply was just as brief: "You're suspended. And you must resign as senior class president." The suspension passed, of course, and years later, memories of high school seem to run together, with a few highs and some corresponding lows standing out from the rest. It was a period that didn't have as much of an effect on my character formation as it does for some persons—perhaps because of my early experiences. The real period of profound change in my life came during my first two years of college. High school, for the most part, was an era of wide horizons and untroubled waters.

An exception was a certain July fourth.

Several of us wanted a fireworks bomb we would long remember, and as it turned out, that is exactly what we got.

I had a can of black powder that I used to fire a Civil War cap-and-ball pistol, and I figured that if a little powder exploded enough to blow a ball out of the pistol, a lot of it should make quite an impressive flash.

I had seen many Saturday matinee western movies where the cowboy poured out a trail of powder on the ground, leading back to the powder keg. When the cowboy lit the powder, he *always* had time to get out of the way of the ensuing blast—even if the trail was short. I followed the movies perfectly, and poured out a short trail for the fuse, leading to the can with the rest of the powder. I figured I'd have time to get out of the way.

I don't know if my powder was super-fast burning or if the movie stuff was doctored to give the pokey cowboys time to get to safety, but when I touched a match to that powder it flashed and exploded immediately, right under my nose. I got the fireworks bomb, all right, but the bomb got me, too.

The explosion burned all exposed skin on my head and hands, and the pain was as if my entire face was being held down on a red hot burner. If Hades is supposed to be eternal fire, then pain such as I felt at that moment should cause everyone in the world to try to avoid it.

What was most serious was my eyes. The pain was intense, and when I tried to open them, I could barely squint. I could see nothing but the etched after-glow of the explosion. I was rushed to the hospital, where the facial burns were treated in the emergency room. The physicians kept shooting me with pain killers, but these didn't seem to quell the intensity of the burning on my face and hands. Finally, a doctor said they could give me no more—too much would be dangerous. I had to just withstand the pain.

They called a specialist in to check my eyes. Though I could still see some light, he was not sure what the eventual damage might be. All I remember is that it felt as if a burning coal was embedded in the iris of each eye.

By the time they had bandaged me like an Egyptian mummy and were rolling me to my room, I was beginning to feel better. I felt reasonably sure that my eyes, even though singed on the lens, would be all right once healed. My skin had suffered only second degree burns with just one small area that had a third degree burn.

It seems that my physical dilemmas have gone in spans of a year, since it took a full year to toughen my skin so the red splotches would blend to an even white pigment—and I wouldn't have to fight the blood blisters that always followed the slightest blow to my face.

I was lucky, to be sure . . . if luck is what it was. The experience could have led to permanent blindness, but my eyes healed perfectly, and my sight was never endangered. In the days that passed before those mummy-like bandages came off I had long thoughts as

Always give a person
a second chance,
but be sure to
explain his mistake.

to what it would be like to live a life in perpetual darkness. When the day came that I was able to use my eyes
once again, I was so relieved I wanted to cry out in
thanksgiving. Now, as I am able to put that experience in
perspective with the other events of my life, I realize that
it was one more instance of being spared for an important task that had not yet been revealed to me.

CHAPTER

3

During the summers of my high school years, I worked in lumber and plywood mills. Physical labor was not new to me. My dad had instilled in me the importance of the work ethic by starting me on summer jobs when I was in the eighth grade. But still, living away from home in a boarding house was both an experience and a responsibility. It was an adventure in that I was on my own for the first time, making and spending my own money. It was a responsibility in that I had to make good.

The initial two weeks on one job gave my hands an awful beating—I started mill work by flipping and turning heavy sheets of plywood when they came out of the sander. The sheets had to be handled on the rough sides and edges, and they were too slick to pick up with gloves, so I constantly had open sores until my hands healed and toughened. The foreman even complained that I was getting blood on the plywood, though he was unable to offer any suggestions as to how I could keep it from happening. Older, more experienced mill workers just did their jobs and gave me no quarter, though a few times I saw flashes of a knowing smirk. I soon learned that this job was the hardest and worst in the plant—just the place to start a green kid to see if he could take it.

I didn't cry "Uncle," and after a week, when the test was over, I could sense the acceptance of the foreman, who had stood a few feet behind me for a large portion of that week—like the hooded man awaiting his call to swing the execution ax.

No matter how tough a task was, I knew I was expected to complete it as a man—and with an eager smile. And being just a kid, I always seemed to draw the worst jobs. I shoveled tar, cleaned the train tracks, swept, fed plywood into the dryer, off-beared the dryer (pulled the plywood panels off the conveyer belt and stacked them), and ran the "gluepete gloop" machine (nickname for the glue mixer). Worst of all was the dreaded chore of unloading the fifty-pound sacks of lime from the rail cars. Lime was used in making the glue, and some of the powder always collected on the outside of the bags. The rail cars were hot and the sweat on my bare arms activated the lime on the bags. As a result, my first layer of skin would be burned off after unloading the lime bags by hand. But I learned to keep my mouth shut and work hard. I had been warned when starting out in the mill that I was to make no mention about a union. I was expected to do my job and ask no questions, and for that I would be paid the princely sum of $2.17 per hour.

The job was no brain burner; they just wanted a warm body that could put out the work.

At the end of each work day, I was exhausted. Returning to the boarding house, I could look forward to a meal of either a creative hot dog dish or hamburger fixed in some exotic down-home way. But what could one expect, paying only twenty bucks per week for a breakfast of bacon and eggs; a lunch of sandwich, fruit, milk, and

dessert; and a dinner of hot dogs, hamburger, potatoes, milk, and a vegetable.

I lived in the attic. You could only stand up straight in the center of the room—at the peak of the roof. The bathroom, commonly shared, was on the main floor. It was a gem of modern plumbing. Many a time I found myself tiptoeing from the bathtub across a floor covered with the refuse from an overflowing toilet.

Other boarders who shared the accommodations included a drunk, who killed himself in an auto wreck while I was there, and a colorful assortment of fellow laborers. The drunk was a particularly sad case; he had been a Marine during World War II and had never recovered from shell shock experienced in the invasion of the Pacific Islands.

Many of these stories I kept to myself, not even telling my parents. They had put me there, and I was determined to succeed. In fact, I wanted to do more than just succeed—I wanted to leave my mark as a hard-working, cooperative young man.

I grew up a lot that first summer after high school, although the experience was nothing compared to my introduction to college and military life at Virginia Polytechnic Institute, at Blacksburg, my dad's alma mater. Little did I know that I was about to enter one of the most life-changing epochs I had ever experienced.

From the earliest days one thought had been drilled into me again and again: Once you start something you stick with it and see it through. That certainly was in my mind as I took on the drudge jobs in the mill— and again as I reported at VPI as a freshman to embark on a program that would lead to a degree and a commission as an Army officer.

VPI in the mid-1960s was a school of about 4,000 men, most of whom were in the Army or Air Force officer candidate programs. The campus, with its imposing gray stone buildings, looked a little like a fortress to me, yet the broad expanse of lawn was inviting. Centrally located were the drill field and lower quadrangle, two areas with which I was to become intimately acquainted as time went on.

Dad had told me his experiences as a student there, and we had laughed about some of the things that had happened to him as a cadet. Those discussions, however, in no way prepared me for what I was about to experience.

Freshmen—or "Rats"—as the first-year cadets were known—arrived two weeks ahead of the returning students for an indoctrination period designed to familiarize us with the military routine of the school. We were issued uniforms, an M-1 rifle, assigned to dorms, and within a very short time after arriving on campus made to believe that a VPI Rat had less status than the dogs that wandered onto the campus from Blacksburg.

Shortly after arrival, at one of the formations, we heard the old standard line from an upperclassman cadet officer who was there to help break us in—or down.

"Look at the man on your right and the one on your left, because come spring they're not going to be here."

He was right.

My first roommate was a good example. Not long after we had started school he asked me:

"Bob, do you think it will get worse?"

"We haven't seen anything yet," I replied. "It's going to get ten times worse."

The next day, when I got back to my room after drill, he was gone. He'd left a note asking me to turn in his M-1 for him, and had just left the campus. Lots of others followed.

But now I was alone. And the next day, Sunday, we were marched as a company into town for church. This

Don't rely completely
on another's advice;
inquire for yourself.
You are the one who
has to live with the
decision.

was our first Sunday and it was quite an inspiration to see the whole corps marching up the main street of town to worship. That afternoon, we were given privileges in the company—a welcome and needed break from the harassment of upperclassmen.

I was sitting on my bed with my head hanging low thinking about my plight. My despair was at its lowest ebb. I felt a hand touch my shoulder. Slowly I raised my head to see a tall, lean, raw-boned farm boy with a broad grin. He stuck out his hand, and in a slow, Southern drawl said: "Hi, I'm Floyd. Floyd Aylor. I'm your new roommate."

We commiserated for a few minutes as we got acquainted, then got on with being VPI cadets. The experiences that followed at the school made us the best of friends and we still see each other constantly, for Floyd is my partner in many business ventures.

At the time you're going through a system of military hazing, it is hard to see justification for some of the treatment. The whole procedure seemed dehumanizing to me—and it was certainly depersonalizing. In the course of a summer, I had gone from the position of senior class president, with many friends, at Portland's Lincoln High, to Rat. R-A-T, actually; these upperclassmen really stressed what it meant to be a Rat.

Once school started, Rat routine became standard. Awake at 4:30 A.M. to begin preparations for the first formation and the PI—police inspection—of the room. Shoes had to be shined, brass buckles, buttons, and insignia were "blitzed," and the entire uniform brushed, then dabbed at with masking tape to get rid of lint. Visors on our caps were rubbed with Vasoline to shine like a mirror. In addition to the uniform, the room had to be in perfect order: bed made so that it would bounce a coin, all clothes hung in the proper sequence and spaced the designated amount, each book placed where

TEDHAINES

it belonged on the shelf, and shoes not being worn put away. And woe be to the Rat who allowed any sign of dust in even the most out-of-the-way places in the room.

Before breakfast we had formation and inspection, and then marched to the mess hall. Rats were required to eat a "square meal"—that is, the utensil carrying food had to be brought up from the plate in a straight line, then across at a ninety-degree angle to the mouth. All this while sitting at attention on the front two inches of the chair. We could speak to upperclassmen only when spoken to, and could not "cut our eyes" (look anywhere but straight ahead).

We Rats slugged our meal down in a hurry and got ourselves excused from the mess hall—so as to avoid any more contact than was necessary with the upperclassmen. As we passed from building to building on campus, we were allowed to walk only on the extreme right six inches of the sidewalk, and there, too, we had to march at attention, not cutting our eyes. Everyone we met on campus had to be greeted with "Good morning, Captain (or whatever the rank), Sir." Even a stray canine was met with "Good morning, Dog, Sir!"

One thing we learned quickly was to spend as much time as possible in our rooms when not in class. Actually, classes were a welcome relief from the military routine, for that was about the only time we could relax. Even in the dorms, however, Rats were fair game for any upperclassman, to be quizzed about anything from the history of VPI to the middle names of the Cadet Corps Officers. Missed answers subjected the freshman to "rat demerits" which had to be worked off by cleaning an upperclassman's room.

Afternoons were for lab classes, drill, and athletic participation—and looking out for upperclassmen. Most of us spent our free moments in our rooms, usually dog tired, though we didn't dare lie down on the bed since the room had to be ready for PI inspection at all times during the day.

The discipline forced upon the freshman cadets was tough, and in the first few weeks of school, many left the campus. I was lucky in that I had a visit by my father, who had come to the area on business.

He came to the campus and arranged for me to get away for a while—even though freshmen were not usually permitted to be off campus during their first term after 7:30 P.M. Dad and I had dinner, went to a movie, and played a game of miniature golf. As we talked, I commented that the hazing was a lot tougher than I had expected it to be.

"I used to laugh when you told me what they did to you, but this isn't funny," I said. "I don't know whether I can take it for the rest of the year."

Dad said the right thing. "Son," he told me, "if you go through this first year, I'll be proud of you."

A simple statement, but it was what I needed to carry me through the remainder of the year. I took all the nonsense the upperclassmen handed out, made acceptable grades, won a gold medal in rope climbing, and was elected Captain of K Company of the Freshman Corps on Rat Day—a time when roles were reversed and we got to treat the upperclassmen to some of the guff they had been giving us.

That freshman year proved the adage "misery loves company," because the Rats soon learned that the only people on campus they could trust were fellow Rats. We were all individuals, from diverse socio-economic backgrounds and with startlingly different interests, but we quickly developed a lasting camaraderie, based in part on our fear of upperclassmen.

Monday nights were the worst night of the academic year, for that was when the upperclassmen held "Rat meetings." We were assembled in a stuffy

You win a war by
putting together the
best equipment and
manpower, coupled
with an imaginative
and workable plan
It is the same in
business.

room, where we braced and took all kinds of verbal abuse from the upperclassmen. Demerits were handed out freely. Sometimes the punishment meant studying at a brace, with the room door open and the room ready for inspection. (A "brace" at VPI meant being able to hold a matchstick between your shoulder blades and under your chin.) Our beds always had to be ready for inspection; in fact, I never slept under the covers, only on top of the bed, with a blanket. That routine made it easier to get ready for the morning check.

Many times that first year at VPI I asked myself "Why" and "What are they trying to prove?" What wasn't clear at the time was that values were being imparted through what seemed like Medieval torture-chamber methods—lasting values such as humility, trust, belief in one's self, and honor. Above all, honor.

Virginia Polytechnic, like the U.S. Service Academies and other military schools, had a strict honor code, and violations of that code could lead to dismissal and "drumming out" of the Cadet Corps.

The code had four basic offenses considered violations: lying, stealing, cheating, and the failure to report another cadet for committing one of those offenses. Cadets had to sign a statement on each paper or examination that the work was his and his alone. The code stated that a cadet who knew of another who had cheated or otherwise violated the code and did not report it was considered as guilty as the original offender, thus making each cadet an informer.

Honor code violators were turned in to the Honor Committee, which then scheduled a hearing, at which the accused had a chance to plead his case, usually with the aid of an upperclassman "defense attorney."

If found guilty of a serious code violation, dismissal was the ultimate punishment—especially if "drumming out" was assessed. That ceremony always took place in the dead of night, before the entire cadet corps. No lights were allowed anywhere on campus—with the exception of the streetlights. These, however, were covered with blankets, like a shroud. It was a chilling effect.

The campus was already quiet since it was past call to quarters and lights out. Senior upperclassmen would go to each room and awaken the cadets, informing them that they were not to talk, but to get dressed in the uniform of the day and assemble for formation in fifteen minutes. After gathering in formation, each company was marched to the lower quadrangle. In the eerie subdued light, with the drummers from the corps band rolling a beat comparable to an impending execution before a firing squad, we felt like we were living a nightmare.

As the sentence was read, the convicted cadet was stripped of his buttons, stripes, and any symbol of the corps or the school. You could sense a sickish feeling creeping up from the pit of your stomach, and you had to dig your nails into the skin of your hands to know that this was real—it was no dream. The corps then did an about face on the disgraced cadet and were ordered never to mention his name again on campus. As far as VPI was concerned, he had not existed, and he would not be permitted to ever return to the campus.

The honor code was just one other aspect of life at VPI that was designed to keep us busy, scared, obedient, and honest. Most of us had to witness only one drumming out to experience all we wanted of the humiliation and fear. That fear turned to paranoia about the honor system during my sophomore year at VPI. Though my obedience to the system was impeccable, I began telling myself that I had to be cautious not to even be *suspected* of any breach of the code. I kept asking myself whether or not the cadet officers would believe my innocence or just decide to make an example of me. The fear preyed

A leader directs the action, is guided by counsel, and is humbled by his followers.

on my mind so much that my grades were affected, and by the end of my sophomore year, I knew I either had to transfer from VPI or say goodbye to any sort of academic credit.

I was hurt, disillusioned, and dismayed, for I was experiencing something that I was unprepared to deal with: failure.

Fortunately, I was accepted for transfer as a junior to Lewis and Clark, a fine liberal arts college in Portland. With the help of a counselor at the University of Oregon Medical School, I was able to begin putting the VPI experience in perspective by the time classes started at Lewis and Clark that fall.

CHAPTER
4

 My junior and senior years at Lewis and Clark College led to graduation with a B.S. degree in Business Administration in 1964. Since I did not live on campus, I was one of those students sometimes referred to as a "day-dodger." I worked hard, both at school and in a part-time job keeping books for a downtown office building in Portland. From my junior year on I paid for my college education.

At Lewis and Clark, academics took on a new perspective for me. Compared to the routine at VPI—where I had little sleep and many hours a day involved in military preparations such as shining brass, drills, and working off demerits—I now had ample time to study, with hours to spare for my job. My grades reflected that attention. It became apparent that the VPI slippage had been temporary, and the emotional trauma was behind me.

After completion of the traditional four years, I went to work for Blyth and Company in Portland, in their account executive training program. Concurrent with my job there, I continued as a full-time student at Lewis and

Ability plus effort
equals achievement.
With less ability
you have to put forth
more effort to reach
the same goal.

Clark, working toward degrees in accounting and economics. I found myself busy every waking moment. I would study in the morning before the market opened, would study during every break and at lunch. Then after work I studied and went to night classes until time for bed. I completed my accounting degree a year later, along with successfully passing all the examinations required to become an account executive.

I knew, however, that it was physically impossible to keep up that kind of pace. I could not pursue my educational goals and maintain a full-time job. So I left Blyth to finish a degree in economics. I became a day student again, and in place of a formal job, began to invest in the stock market. For years I had been steeped in the art and science of investing. Now it was time to apply this accumulated knowledge.

The stock training dated back to those early teen-age years when my father would come into my bedroom with the *Wall Street Journal* or *Standard and Poor's Business Index* to teach me about stocks and bonds and how to evaluate a company. I had also taken the New York Institute of Finance course on Brokerage Procedure and the University of Wisconsin's course in Investment Banking by correspondence while attending college—both of which helped buoy me as I made the plunge.

Everything fit together perfectly. The stock investments rendered reward, with the profits allowing me to finish my education at Lewis and Clark and see me through an MBA degree at the University of Portland. Whether by divine guidance or blind luck or uncommon skill, those investments matured with handsome profits. And just before the market down-turn in the late 1960s, I sold my holdings for investment in another venture. Timing couldn't have been better to get out of stocks and to seek timberlands in the South—as both an investment and an adventure.

Fortunately, I knew just the person to help me with this new venture. Outfitted with a high sense of purpose and with my educational pursuits at bay, I went to Georgia with the same optimism many an immigrant Englishman had on his mind in the 1800s—"to ranch the colonies."

Sylvania, Georgia, a small town on the Savannah River midway between Augusta and Savannah, would hardly seem a mecca for real estate investment, but for a young man who had hunted throughout the area as a child and who had an idea that Southern pine could mean gold—green gold—it was the logical place to go.

A big part of that reason was Jerry Manack.

Jerry, a solid, swarthy-complexioned woodsman of Italian extraction, had been a friend and hunting companion for many years. He was the kind of hunter for whom a rifle or shotgun becomes an extension of sight. Hunting, though, was not Jerry's only talent. He was a natural woodsman, personally and professionally, and it was with him that I was able to invest in Georgia timberlands.

Jerry was as much a part of Sylvania as he was of the pine stands near town, for Sylvania was as solidly conservative and "down home" as Jerry. Anyone who has traveled on the back roads of America has been in a Sylvania, Georgia, whether it be in the South, the midlands, the Oklahoma panhandle, the vast reaches of Dakota territory, or on the steppes of the Sierra Nevada.

A town of 3600 God-fearing, Bible-thumping souls, Sylvania had a main street with its one signal light, the dry goods store, an old-fashioned drugstore, and the county courthouse, since it is the county seat of Screven County. The town's angled parking spaces were filled with pickup trucks interspersed with Cadillacs and Lincolns, the latter vehicles representing the farmers and retired moonshiners who had "made it."

Buy for value (what
is owned less what
is owed) and earning
power. An asset is
worthless if it can't
earn anything, and
earnings are risky
if you pay more than
an asset is worth.

Jerry had a unique way of valuing a timber tract. He would just walk through different sections and count each tree that, in his judgment, would be worth a twenty-dollar bill.

"See that tree?" he would say. "That's worth a twenty-dollar bill. All you have to do is look around you and count the twenty-dollar bills." But that was just part of it; the other was jawing with the owners, usually local farmers. Fortunately, we could both go into any home in the backwoods of rural Georgia and talk with the folks. Talk country.

It was not put on for either of us. Jerry was a native of that area, and I had spent enough time there to know something of the land and its people. Besides, my upbringing on Grandmother's farm and in the apartment house in Augusta had blessed me with the ability to be comfortable with persons of all walks of life, from a Georgia sharecropper or swamp rat to those in the board room of a major corporation. It was a trait that I valued.

Our procedure was relatively simple, following a theory that anyone else could have used. It was primarily based on searching out lands that had been committed to the government-planted-pine program some years back. We calculated that those trees were about five years away from maturing in size from a pulpwood value to saw timber value. Pulpwood value was about half that of saw timber, so in theory, only about five years was needed before the pines would double in value. In addition, we wanted property that had a good stand of mature timber. Since the mature timber was usually located deep in the swamp part of a property, it was in many cases overlooked by other potential buyers—because of the dangers ever present in those areas.

Our goal, then, was to purchase the land and timber for what we felt we could sell a cutting contract on the mature timber and the value of the planted pines at pulp prices. Our next step was to sell the mature timber, and then present the property to investors priced in terms of land value and the potential of the planted pines when they reached saw timber size in five years. It was a system that usually rewarded us with one-hundred percent profit over the original price.

Jerry always was more comfortable in the field than I was, and more than once stopped me from stepping on a rattler that I had not seen. One day in particular, in the middle of summer, mosquitos were so thick they nearly blinded us, and we had to keep our mouths closed to avoid an early lunch. That day Jerry saved me from possible snakebite three times—each time I was about to step on or walk into a rattler or moccasin.

"Never give a moccasin a chance," he would tell me. "They have a nasty temperament—just love to bite you." But he followed up with, "Now don't be afraid of 'em, either. Just hit 'em in the head with a good hickory stick."

He used to carry that hickory stick with him everywhere in the woods, and when the snake was longer than the stick, he would instruct me to keep the snake's attention and say, "I'll sneak behind it and pop it one." Sometimes I felt like just so much dangled bait. Fortunately, Jerry never missed. One of the unique ways he would avoid any snake that might want to take a swim with us when we would take our after-work bath in Briar Creek was simply to duck under water. Jerry reasoned that a snake can't bite you under water or it would drown. Thankfully, I never had opportunity to test the theory.

As I have stated before, I sincerely feel that I was given these investment opportunities for a purpose— just as I felt that my life had been spared through serious accidents and illnesses for a reason.

The Georgia land investment was profitable for a number of reasons. But we always selected our lots carefully, and always paid each owner a fair price for his land.

Names (important people) don't solve problems; ideas solve problems.

(One owner, I remember, said he would sell only if we gave him cash and a new Lincoln. We gave him the cash all right, but he bought his own Lincoln.)

I decided that same philosophy could work with farm lands in Oregon, and upon my return to the Northwest in the late 1960s, began looking for farms that might be made profitable in the Willamette Valley and regions between the valley and the Oregon coast.

With any venture involving buying and selling where substantial amounts of investment capital are involved, timing can be crucial. As I began buying farms and acreages in Oregon, I realized that once again my fortunes were being guided.

During this period Oregon had not yet experienced the land boom that was to follow in the mid-seventies, when wealthy individuals and investment companies bought much of the open land on speculation. I found willing sellers at fair prices, particularly with marginal properties that needed attention. On these properties, I was able to lease the cultivation rights while still holding title, making it profitable for the lessee and for my company. Field crops, row crops, and nut tree orchards were all part of the land purchases of that period.

This was a period of adventure for me in the business world, and in my recreational life as well. I was on the verge of living an experience that had once been only a childhood daydream.

I guess it is common for a child to fantasize drama and even heroism, and I was no exception. In fact, when I was little I would often dress in an outfit that I felt was appropriate for my chosen hero of the day. One time I might be a lone cowboy heading off a band of marauding Indians and another day an adventurer in the jungles of Africa—helping Tarzan save a defenseless safari from wild animals or menacing natives.

But during the summer months, when the moist

Georgian air was heavy with heat and even the breezes through the windows were warm and nearly suffocating, I would think about my special exploit: big game hunting.

It is an odd thing, but a good portion of this fantasy came true. As a boy of twelve, I spent the summer with Indians in Canada, hunting with my father. We were located in Northern Canada, isolated from civilization by hundreds of miles, just my father, me, the Indians, and our horses. It was a glorious adventure. We spent each day climbing mountains, tracking animals, and living off the land. Few youngsters can claim to have killed a moose when just twelve.

But the complete fulfillment of my childhood reverie came when I was in my late twenties, along the Mara River in Kenya. I had gone to Africa on a hunting safari, especially in hopes of facing some of the big five (lion, elephant, buffalo, rhino, and leopard). For days we tracked in the shadows of leopard and lion, but could not place ourselves in the correct position to gain a shot. We followed up on all the rumors from the natives, scouting the plains and the timbered areas, or sitting long hours by baited traps.

On one occasion we situated ourselves at the end of a dried wash to head off three lions supposedly moving that way. We must have been desperate for action. In retrospect I realize that where the guide and I stationed ourselves gave us only a quick running shot before the lions would be on us. My 375 bolt-action rifle would count for but one shot and his 470 Nitro Express double rifle could be fired twice. Three shots for three confused, prowling, angry lions. The longer I waited the more I realized that this fantasy might turn into a disaster—my disaster.

We stood our ground, and I quietly let out a sigh of relief when the lions did not show.

Always leave some-
thing on the table.
The best deal is
where both sides
make a profit.

But the real test—and the complete fulfillment of my boyhood daydream—came two weeks into the safari. We were hunting the fiercest and most deadly big game in Africa, the African buffalo. He has earned this distinction because of his explosive temper and his ability to absorb high-powered bullets and still escape or muster a deadly charge. He is black, with an almost slick hairless skin, weights about a ton, stands five feet high at the shoulder, and carries those deadly horns, which can measure five feet from point to point, like a loaded arsenal ready for action. He is truly a death machine—but a highly intelligent one. By continually circling, a wounded buffalo will often confuse a tracker and lie in hiding until the hunter approaches—and then charge without warning. Unlike most animals, he is endowed with acute sensitivity in all of the senses. He can smell you, he can see you, he can hear you. And he has the intelligence to use these senses to his advantage—not necessarily to retreat but to position himself to run those deadly ebony horns clean through you.

For days we had been hunting for a trophy buffalo. The region had been experiencing a drought, and grass was sparse. As a result the game was spread thin.

At dawn one morning a group of Masai men wearing rough cotton togas and carrying spears appeared on the trail and began telling us in their native tongue about a nearby herd of buffalo that contained several large bulls. We were skeptical. On other occasions these "leads" had resulted in long, fruitless treks through jungles and over hot dusty plains.

The area they were talking about, however, did sound promising. It was thickly wooded and close to good grazing. The principal ingredients for a likely buffalo habitat seemed in place: lots of food and an easy escape to the woods if the animals sensed danger.

After conferring with our trackers, we decided to

scout the herd. As quietly as possible we moved cautiously through the grass and toward the trees where the Masai had directed us. My senses were switched to super-acute, tingles jumped up my spine, and large goose bumps formed on my arm as an involuntary shudder rippled through my body. I was excited—and scared. The climactic moment was near. I could feel it. I just knew that in a few minutes I would come face to face with something that would want to kill me and easily could if given a chance.

As we emerged from the first clump of trees into an opening in thick brush, we could see two fine bulls trailing a herd of cows and calves. The bulls had stopped momentarily to see what was following them. The guide studied the animals through his binoculars, leaned over, and whispered that I should try for the one in front, bigger of the two. He looked at me, his eyes hard. "Shoot him behind the foreleg in the heart, and don't make a bad shot of it. If you wound him we have to track him down."

I knew what he meant. Tracking a wounded buffalo is like playing Russian roulette. You are on his home territory and he is mad—mad with a fury that will not end until he has totally destroyed those who made him angry. In this case, me.

I took a deep breath, lined the cross hairs at the right spot, and squeezed the trigger. The report of the rifle, the shock of the recoil, and the smack of the bullet as it hit the tough hide of the buffalo all came at once. I quickly ejected the spent shell and rammed home another live cartridge. I was ready for a second shot. The guide threw up his hands to wave off my intention.

"The companion bull has moved in front of yours— let's see what happens!"

The bulls began to move off together, disappearing into the woods. I had missed the vital spot. The buffalo

TED HAINES

was only wounded. There was nothing anyone could say—we had no choice but to follow.

My stomach churned. I felt dreadful that I had not put home that first shot. The bitter taste of bile jarred me into the realization that my life was on the line. My heart was pumping so hard I could barely catch my breath. One mistake—just one mistake—and I was a dead man.

I followed in the footsteps of the guide, but it was like walking in a haze with a foggy kaleidoscope of colors all around. I had the distinct sense that I was falling—falling into some deep abyss. Was this how it felt just before you died? I didn't have time to speculate.

"There he is!"

The cry of the guide wrenched me back to reality. Now I could see the bull. His magnificent head was thrashing from side to side, brandishing a fine set of horns, polished, pointed, and brutal.

The bull lowered his head and started to move through the thicket. I brought up my rifle—tried to sight him into my scope—but all I could see was blurry limbs and tall grass. I kept following in the direction of movement and finally got a fix on a black spot between two trees. I fired rapidly, knowing that it had to be the buffalo, but what part of his body, I was not sure. I jammed in another cartridge and fired again as the black spot continued to move. And then the round was over. He had moved out of sight.

We followed the bull for quite some time, realizing that he was getting sicker and meaner as the minutes passed. He was carrying at least one bullet—and possibly two more. Nothing that would sweeten his personality.

The woods began to open into small clearings dotted by thick clumps of brush. Our African trackers were close to us now. The bull's trail was clear and I think they sensed that he was near.

They were right. Just as we rounded a thicket we saw him watching us from a tight clearing. The buffalo just stood there, waiting. We knew that when we were all in view he would charge. The gun-bearer handed me the rifle. I raised it, took careful aim, and squeezed the trigger—only to hear a click rather than the roar of gunpowder. The gun had dry fired. In all the excitement, neither the gun-bearer nor I had realized that I had a spent round in the chamber. The guide threw up his rifle and fired a head shot that pierced the buffalo's horns and turned his head.

Now the buffalo's attention was directed squarely at me. He lowered his head. "Look out!" the guide yelled, "He's going to charge!"

As I reached for another cartridge I realized that the gun-bearer, the guide, and everyone else in the party were running for cover. I was facing the wounded buffalo alone. As the beast readied his charge, I shoved the shell into the chamber, brought the rifle up, and fired, dropping him where he stood.

That night we ate oxtail soup and boiled buffalo tongue. The guide and others in the party asked me why I had stood my ground, when discretion at that point said cut and run. To this day I'm not entirely sure why. I do know I had rehearsed just such a scene in my mind, in my bed in Georgia when I was a child. It happened just like my daydream—I had decided I would not run, but stand—all alone if necessary.

It was only afterward, when I came to understand how vulnerable I really was in the face of that sinewed fury, that I realized I might have been tap-dancing with the Prince of Fate once too often. Yet I had been spared.

And again I wondered, why? I knew it was for some greater reason than fulfilling the daydream of a small Georgia boy.

My life was going well. I had been given recognition for community and academic service, including an honorary doctorate from the the University of Portland, and a Distinguished Alumnus award from Lewis and Clark. Appointments by the Governor of Oregon and the President of the United States to important commissions were high points of my civic activities at the time.

But everything else pales in comparison with one particular highlight: meeting and marrying Marilyn Hooper. It has been a fairy-tale romance—and yet a beautiful reality. Her tender understanding and gracious acceptance of each of life's daily challenges makes me *know* that every day will be a success. With a confidence I find hard to even express, I know that we were placed in each other's care for a reason. I don't want to even guess what reason the Lord might have . . . I am only thankful for His gift to me.

I had everything a man could ask for. A loving wife and two pretty, healthy daughters, the respect of my parents, business success, and recognition for public service.

I couldn't remember a time of greater euphoria and fulfillment.

Then one day Marilyn noticed what looked like a speck of tar on my leg.

CHAPTER

5

"Bob, what is that on your leg? It looks like a bit of tar. What did you get on you?"

"Oh, it isn't anything, Marilyn, just a mole. It's been there a while. There's nothing to worry about."

Or was there?

For years I had heard and read about the seven danger signals of cancer, and I knew one sign was a mole that changed color. That had now happened with the small mole on the front of my right leg, just below the knee.

Even so, I wasn't particularly worried. If it was a "bad" mole, it could just be cut out, and the problem would be gone. After all, I had never heard of anyone dying from a cancerous mole—only from the much publicized leukemia and lung cancer. I figured a mole had to be low on the cancer worry list, and certainly not a life or death concern. I suppose I knew I might be rationalizing a bit at that point, and I can remember one night while driving home I reached down and felt the mole through my pants leg, thinking it might have gone away. That was wishful thinking, for it hadn't.

Marilyn and I had just returned from Hawaii. It had been a vacation for "the two of us." No business pressures, no phone calls, and no kids. While we missed the girls, it was nice to have some time alone for change.

I wanted to get all the sun possible in Hawaii, but carelessly tried to make up for Oregon's bleak winter skies in one day. And I was paying the price. Severely sunburned, my skin peeled in massive strips, painfully exposing a tender underlayer. I glowed with the heat of a well-turned suckling pig just off the spit—with a skin color to match.

Once home, my blotchy red-and-tan skin returned to normal, and life fell into the usual level of activity. It was about a month after our trip that Marilyn commented on the mole.

As time passed, the mole maintained its ebony color, and though it didn't hurt, it continued to grow irregularly. Marilyn insisted that I see a doctor. I kept putting off making an appointment, hoping that the mole was not a serious problem. Deep down, though, I felt a hard-to-explain uneasiness. I didn't want to go to the doctor but . . . I finally yielded. Now, as I sat in the small cubicle looking at the padded examination table covered with a long strip of paper, some of the horror stories I had read as a child and had seen at the movies rushed through my mind like rain clouds tumbled by a Pacific storm. The images were so vivid. I could hear the shrieks of pain from wretched prisoners on the rack. I could hear the skitter of rats across a stone floor—anxious to sink their razor teeth into the shriveled flesh of the prisoner chained against the dungeon wall.

I could see, also, the nameless creatures who stared into space—their expressionless eyes fixed on some unknown shape of darkness—some psychological agony that might even transcend physical pain. It was the agony of not knowing what would happen next or how severe the pain might be. How could they have survived—and why would they want to?

It was a long ten minutes in that sterile cubicle. Then Dr. Shields burst in. This is a man I'd seen socially on several occasions, but here, on his turf, in his white smock—he was another person.

"H'lo, Bob, what seems to be the trouble?"

I told him about the mole—minimizing my concerns, of course. I wouldn't have bothered at all except for the fact that my wife had insisted.

"Good for her," he said. "Now, let's have a look."

Doc Shields checked the mole carefully, then fired off a volley of questions.

How long had I had the mole?

When did I notice the changes?

How much had it grown?

He didn't say anything that gave away his feelings or conclusions. Just before wheeling around to leave the room, he barked a parting command: "Wait here a minute. I want my partner to have a look at this, too."

Right then I realized for the first time that "the speck of tar" might be more serious than I had allowed myself to believe. Still, though, it was hard for me to accept that a tiny mole—even one that was growing— could be a critical threat. After all, I was in my thirties, in good physical shape, the fabled "prime of life."

Doc returned in a few minutes, and introduced me to his partner. They both looked at the mole, and then started throwing medical jargon back and forth, ignoring me completely except for that piece of discolored flesh that absorbed their attention.

By now, sweat poured from my armpits. I had had a lot of experience with doctors over the years, and I knew that when they talked this way, leaving the patient out of the conversation, it was serious. I got more and more nervous. Finally, they began to talk in layman's language.

"Bob, this could be a cancerous mole," Doc Shields told me, "but we don't think so. We're just not sure, though, so what we have to do is excise it, and send it into the pathology lab for biopsy. We'll let the lab boys tell us what we're dealing with. We can take it out right here."

I have to admit I was relieved, because I had had enough time to worry about the mole, and cancer in any form was not something I wanted to deal with. So they cut out the mole, stitched up the incision, and I went on my way. I was scheduled to return in a week to have the stitches out and get the report from the pathology lab.

I really wasn't very worried that week. If it had been *that* serious, wouldn't they have told me? And yet . . . there was that chance—that awful chance. Only that coldly impersonal lab report could tell me. There was nothing I could do until it was ready. So I played golf and went on with life as usual.

I still was confident when I returned to Doc's office the following week to get the stitches removed. When I left home that morning I really didn't feel that this day would be any different than any other in my life, and considered the problem of the mole now behind me.

The routine at Doc's office was just as it had been the week before: the wait . . . the out-of-date *Time* magazines . . . the sterile walls . . . the stiff paper on the examination table . . . the battle with an overactive imagination. It wasn't long before my cool confidence had melted into something resembling anxiety.

The waiting was the worst. I remember wondering if that's how it felt to have an audience with the Pope.

Finally—after what seemed like an unbelievably long wait—Doc Shields blew into the room like he'd been shoved.

He wasted no time on tactful niceties.

"Well, Bob, you've got a melanoma."

"Melanoma?" I frowned. "What's that?"

"It's a cancerous mole. Let me tell you what we're going to do. We're going to cut this wide area, about like so, and if we're lucky, that will get it all."

As he talked, he lightly scribed an oval shape on the front of my leg, around the small incision where the mole had been. It looked like it was about four inches across. He continued to describe the procedure:

"We'll cut that out, and then we'll put in a patch off your leg up here for a skin graft. What we take out we'll send back to pathology, and they'll cut it into small sections and examine it all through a microscope to see if there are any cancer cells."

Melanoma ... cancer ... incision ... pathology. I was hearing what Doc was saying—but not believing. He kept talking and talking. They were going to look for cancer cells. If they didn't get it all with the first operation, they would have to go back and remove my lymph glands. And then there was chemotherapy—tying off my leg and flushing it out with chemicals.

All I could think about was that stupid little mole! All this for a speck of tar!

Doc was still talking about lymph glands and procedures when one phrase seared into my consciousness the way a rancher's branding iron burns a calf.

It was "cure rate."

"Wait a minute," I wanted to scream. "If he's talking about 'cure rate,' that means there are times when this thing isn't curable."

After Doc finished explaining the surgical procedure, I found myself nodding with agreement—like a small child confiding with blind trust in a parent. His nurse made an appointment for me to go into the hospital at the next available date. I quickly realized that hospitals have their schedules of occupancy like hotels, and you can't just move someone out of a room—or off of an operating table—to suit your convenience.

As I left the clinic, my mind was still in a blur. It seemed that all my dreams of enjoying life—and yes, as in the fairy tales, living happily ever after—had been dashed against a rock, the pieces scattered in every direction. My movements were like a robot—mechanical, without feeling. As I slipped into the seat of the car, tears began to well in my eyes. I caught a blurred glimpse of myself in the mirror and it was as if I was fading out of focus. Was that what life and death were all about? One minute everything is in sharp focus—and then you fade from view—as though you had never existed?

I finally managed to move the car out of the parking place and onto the street. It was amazing how the simple mental demands of driving pushed the cold dread from my mind. Even though I wanted to think about my plight, my attention was constantly diverted by the traffic, where I was going, what I was doing. That's how I'll beat this, I told myself, I'll keep busy—every moment—and won't give myself time to think. But each time I would find myself without action, at a traffic light, my eyes would water—glimpses of the children, my wife, and our happy life together would sweep past.

The day of the operation was September third. My birthday. Most people would think, "what a birthday present," but I didn't really care. Surgery was one step closer to putting cancer behind me. On the operating table, before the sodium pentothal put me to sleep, I managed to sit up for a moment. With a groggy voice and thick tongue I murmured, "Doc, thanks for operating on me. Make me well."

My next conscious thought was waking up in the recovery room. I was cold as a dead man, and my body was placed on what felt like a slab of marble. As my mental faculties began to return, I moved my hand gradually down my hip to see if they had removed my leg. I had a preconceived notion that if the cancer had spread they would remove my leg to restrict its advance. I was relieved to touch my upper leg but still I had to muster all my concentration to wiggle my toes—just to be sure that the lower leg was intact, too. This knowledge alone made me feel better.

When I returned to the room, Marilyn was waiting. She whispered that the doctor was ninety-nine percent certain that all the cancer had been removed—from what he could see, the excised area was clean. I felt vastly relieved.

The doctor's visit the next day brought home more of the insidious nature of cancer.

"The problem is, Bob, that if we missed just one cell, if one got away and has reached the lymph glands or another part of the body, then the whole chain could start over again. We've sent the section to pathology, and we'll keep you in here for a few days while we wait for your recovery. This will enable us to look at the results before we release you."

They say that medical students taking pathology begin to imagine symptom after symptom of some of the diseases they encounter. I could certainly relate to this phenomenon. I felt a bulge in my esophagus and immediately they rushed me to have an upper body scan and a barium test to determine whether there was cancer in other parts of the body. This, of course, made me worry all the more. What if my body was infested with cancer? How long would I have? Toward the end of the week we became very anxious about the pathology report, for this was going to really tell the tale.

The report came in the afternoon on the sixth day. Doctor Shields walked into the room and matter of factly stated that the report showed the area to be clean. What glorious news! It was like a huge boulder being lifted from my chest.

Once is not always,
and twice is not
forever.

It wasn't until later that I found out that the boulder had only been shifted, not removed. I was to be subjected to multiple examinations for the next five years in order to make sure that the cancer had really been removed. So, regardless of the lab report, for the next six months I had to visit the doctor, at first weekly, and then every two weeks. At each examination he would check my lymph glands for swelling—a sign of cancer spreading—and examine the incision for any lesions that also would indicate that the murderous cells had escaped the scalpel.

To me, going in for those weekly visits was almost like going before a judge for sentencing. If the cancer had spread, he could pronounce the sentence of death for me. If it had not, I was going to live for another week. Each day became very precious, especially those immediately after an examination. I was thankful for that week of grace and would tell myself that I would live another week. But as the end of the week approached, my week of life was used up—and I wondered if I would be given another week's reprieve.

After six months, I was able to spread the time between visits to two weeks, then, gradually, a month between office calls, and finally every six months. Once past the weekly visits, the goal became a five-year game plan: five years without any sign of the cancer and I was considered to be cured.

At age thirty-five, with everything in life to look forward to, I recognized for the first time that death could very well lurk in my near future—instead of the long life for which I had worked, planned, and dreamed.

I was crushed. Some people with cancer have been told they have only a specific time to live, once the disease has spread beyond control of the physicians. The initial shock must be devastating. But once said, it is over, and it becomes a question of acceptance or rejection of the prognosis. In my case, each visit to the doctor was one in which my anxiety level nearly went off the top of the chart, for each week I didn't know whether I could expect to live or die. It was like a condemned man being buckled to the electric chair—only to receive a governor's pardon at the last possible moment.

These things have a way of continually preying on a normal existence. For intermingled with the pressure of visiting the doctor, I had to have a suspicious lesion removed a few days before Christmas during that first year. Then I had to wait until after Christmas for the pathology report. Fortunately it proved to be benign. But what a miserable Christmas! This emotional roller coaster rolled on and on—for five years.

Mingled with the pressure, anxiety, and dread, however, was the firm knowledge that I had two armies doing battle for me—one earthly and one heavenly. The earthly army, of course, was the hospital and the doctors.

But the other army was even more important.

Many, many friends—brothers and sisters in Christ—were crying out to God on my behalf.

I am confident of two things as I look back on those days: I do believe that God answered our earnest prayers. And I do believe that God spared me to do good for His kingdom. He has a use for me! And He impressed on me the importance of keeping myself right with Him—for after death it is too late.

But I guess there will always be questions.

Why me? Why was I saved? For what purpose has God spared me from this test—and from others that have come in my life?

One thing is clear, as I reflect in these later years. God has loved me enough to apply shock treatment directly to the soul. His direction for my life has come in serious jolts that have forced me from dependence on self back into a trust relationship with Him. In pain and pressure and fear, I have remembered faith. In darkness, I have seen an unfailing light.

"Why spared?"

"Why blessed?"

He knows the reason and He loves me. And that is enough.

CHAPTER

6

"Like father, like son."

Sure, it's a cliché. But there is a lot of truth in that phrase just the same.

It is also true that many sons want to make their own mark, or maybe try to do something a little bit better than their fathers. If that is the challenge, they may choose a totally different avenue from the one which brought fame and fortune to the previous generation.

I've encountered a number of people who believe it is hard to start with a naked idea and see it grow into an irrefutable success. I have never doubted that possibility for one moment! Yes, it takes imagination and—doubly yes—lots of old-fashioned, roll-up-your-sleeves hard work. But it can be done. And believe me, that kind of success is worth more than any other—because it is something you have done on your own.

My father started in business with a small lumber wholesaler, where he became the fifth office employee. He spent his entire career with the same company, rising to President and Chairman of the Board. When he retired, Georgia-Pacific Corporation had sales and profits that made it one of the leaders of the forest products industry. He continues to be lauded as a genius in business finance and management, and deservedly so.

Now, I would be the first to agree that that is a hard act to follow. But it was never my intention to pile rocks on Everest so I could claim to have climbed a little higher. At the same time, however, I didn't feel I should *avoid* a career in business just because my father's record was so outstanding. I am proud and even a braggart about my father's achievement, yet I have itched to be accepted as a successful entrepreneur in my own right, a difficult goal for a son who finds himself in the shadow of an accomplished father.

How, then, was I to leave my own footprints in the cement of American industry? I knew in my heart there was only one way: through creativity and innovation.

That quest led me to Twelve Oaks Farm.

My "El Dorado" is a story that involves some luck, some good horse sense (not mine, I will be quick to add), considerable faith in people, some incredible timing—and a legend.

For several years Marilyn and I had owned a farm near Newberg, Oregon. It was both a retreat and a working producer of filberts. Some time back I decided I wanted a riding horse at the farm for my enjoyment and that of the family.

A friend suggested I ought to look into cutting horses—highly trained and skilled animals that are used to isolate a single cow or calf from a herd. While a number of cutting horses are working ranch stock, many others are used strictly in competition for large purse money, similar to that of race horses. The logic was that it didn't cost any more to keep a cutter, and the investment might pay off well. Besides, they are a marvel to ride when properly trained.

The search for the right horse took me to Pleasant Hill, Oregon, and a stable managed by Carmen and Norm Bryant. The Bryants both were established cutting horse trainers who were winning regularly in Oregon, Northwest, and Pacific Coast cutting horse competitions. They had a horse that I liked, and agreed to teach me to ride. As I got to know the Bryants they shared with me their dream to someday breed and train superior cutting horses.

After one of my lessons at their ranch, Norm asked me to visit with them over some hot tea.

"Bob," he began, "people have made it big in raising and showing cutting horses." Norm stopped talking and looked down at his cup of tea, turned the spoon over with his fingers and then continued. "Purses at the big shows are very high—they can share a purse of over a million dollars at the National Futurity. That's not going to happen to everyone, but let me tell you something that could be just as exciting."

I had been listening patiently, but now I thought it was the time to put in my two cents worth.

"Norm, riding horses is fun, but I don't want to get involved any deeper unless there is a profit to be made. A hobby, to my way of thinking, should also make money. It may sound a little weird, but that's just the way I feel about it."

Norm had impressed me as a quiet man with an easy smile and a ranch drawl. Personable, but not very excitable. I was beginning to see a new side of him as he continued to talk about cutting horses—and how he would go about making money in this business.

His eyes were twinkling bright, his slow drawl had picked up several speed levels—and he was gesturing so enthusiastically with his hands than anyone could have become infected. I must admit that by the time the discussion ended I too was being caught up in his ardor.

No one is an expert
in everything. Be
wise enough to
admit your short-
comings. People will
admire your wisdom
and humility. Then
hire experts to fill
the gaps.

As I rose to leave, he said, "Take this magazine with you. It tells about the greatest sire of cutting horses that ever lived, *Doc Bar.* A dentist bought him for little or nothing. Many of his offspring went on to become national champions. They get a fancy price for breeding and he is worth a fortune now." I took the magazine and that night as I read the article I became a believer.

Over the next few months we began to plan the future of Twelve Oaks Farm. And as we put the ingredients together, the plan became a reality. The stallion we selected for breeding purposes was a son of Doc Bar. But the stallion's dam was also special; she was Annie Glo, a mare who was highly respected for her consistent wins, no matter who was riding her. She also was a champion.

So this three-year-old stallion, Doc's Superstar Bar, became our pride and joy. He was a handsome, bright bay horse with a refined head, short ears, clean, graceful throatlatch, and a deep chest. At 14.2 hands and 1100 pounds, Superstar was a balanced, tightly-structured athlete, with lots of muscle definition in the shoulders and hindquarters. In addition, he showed agility, quickness, and lots of "cow sense"—very important qualities in a cutting horse. And he had charisma, a rare trait of self-pride not found in every horse.

Without question, on paper we were purchasing one of the outstanding young cutting horse stallions in the nation! Doc's Superstar Bar still was a gamble, however, because, at three, he had not proven his ability as a sire and had not been tested in the cutting arena. The youngster was also behind in his training due to an earlier injury.

At Twelve Oaks, we developed a breeding farm where the best of care could be provided for resident broodmares and mares brought in for stud service. The Bryants took a course in breeding at Colorado State University, and after Doc's Superstar Bar was shipped to

TED HAINES

Oregon, our program was launched.

Superstar's first foals were born in 1979, and quickly began proving what the Bryants had felt about the stallion. Norm Bryant said:

"People began telling us that they were the most sensible, trainable colts they ever had. What we were seeing was that his colts were uniform athletes. Even out of different kinds of mares, you could pick his colts. They were good-headed, strong-legged, very stout in the hips, with nice necks and good muscle definition ... hard and strong looking. And the best thing is that every colt I've started on cattle has been real 'cowy.' I've broken colts all my life, but these colts are in the top five percent of all I've ever ridden!"

"Cowy" or "cow sense" is one of the attributes a trainer looks for in a good cutting horse prospect. Besides needing to be superb athletes, cutting horses must possess the inherited ability to outthink the cow. Horses either have it or they don't. It simply isn't something a trainer can teach. Superstar had a tremendous amount of cow sense—and he was passing it along to all his foals!

Although the emphasis at Twelve Oaks was on breeding mares, Superstar's own training continued. We showed him on a limited basis in 1978. And how did he do in his first appearance in a competitive arena? Superstar lived up to his name—and walked away with the Reserve Junior Cutting Championship.

In ten shows that year he won six firsts and three seconds, and ended the year as the Oregon Quarter Horse Association Champion Junior Cutting Horse. In 1979 he placed well in several senior registered cutting classes, and earned the NCHA Certificate of Ability.

It was in 1979 that Superstar's progeny began to shine. One of his first foals, Candee's Hot Sox, was Champion Weanling Filly in three Oregon shows.

Another blessing in the development of Superstar's reputation occurred that year when his dam, Annie Glo, became NCHA World Champion Mare. Although she was sixteen years old and pregnant, she qualified for her induction into the NCHA Hall of Fame. Such a fact did not go unnoticed by the cutting horse world, for now Twelve Oaks Farm was getting bookings from Canada, Minnesota, Idaho, Arizona, Oregon, Montana, California, Washington, and Nevada. Before Superstar's colts were even old enough to start on cattle they were selling for up to ten times the breeding fee.

We had built a great horse farm. Together we had planned, we had sloshed through the mud during the winter the buildings were being constructed, we had hammered nails, dug fence post holes, stretched wire, bought broodmares, raised offspring, traveled across the country, and—most important—prayed.

In 1982 we sold Superstar for more than $800,000. Considering that the horse was purchased for $30,000 in 1977, this has to be seen as a remarkable success story in itself. But the stallion had more than paid his way with breeding fees while I owned him and the offspring he provided me from the broodmares of Twelve Oaks meant a second large profit.

Today when Norm and I kick up our heels and jaw, our conversation inevitably comes around to Superstar and Twelve Oaks. It would be easy enough to sit around and pat ourselves on the back—but that's not the direction our thoughts usually run. We share an unshakable conviction that what happened was the work of God.

"Too many things have happened," Norm will say, "things out of our control, that shot the operation down the road. Luck only goes so far! I feel we have been honest, and have tried to give horsemen the best possible deal when working with us. But we just haven't had the problems that often go along with a developing horse

Don't have someone
do something that
you are not willing
to do.

Share your rewards
with those who have
helped you. It will
return to you tenfold.

operation. I can't help but feel strongly that Someone was looking out for us."

For their commission in promoting the sale of Doc's Superstar Bar, I gave the Bryants a check for more than $200,000. Norm was genuinely surprised by the gesture, but I wouldn't have had it any other way. Twelve Oaks began with a shared commitment—a shared dream. I have always felt that if someone works hard to help you achieve success, you should share that success with him. Had it not been for Carmen and Norm, Twelve Oaks and Doc's Superstar Bar might have been a success story that never happened.

The Bryants and I were all eager to remember—and honor—God's role in the venture. Apart from His grace and blessing, true success is little more than an empty dream.

CHAPTER
7

Not long ago, a friend told me an experience he once had while returning to Portland on a flight from Washington, D.C. In many ways his story reveals the essence of my personal philosophy.

My friend, John, was seated next to a young man dressed in an expensive business suit. It became obvious that the man was extremely frightened by the flight. His anxiety grew to near frenzy when the aircraft encountered turbulence over the Rockies. Pale and wild-eyed, he gripped the armrests of his seat as though he expected to fall from the skies at any moment.

John, who had been reading, thought perhaps he could ease his seat companion's mind with conversation, and they began talking about a variety of subjects. When they discussed their professions, the nervous passenger said he was a civilian inspector with the U.S. Air Force, and that he traveled to different air bases all over the world—mostly by airplane. But he confessed he was deathly afraid of flying!

Curious as to why someone would continually

Everyone wants to belong. That is all motivation is: making people believe they belong, are wanted, and important.

subject himself to what seemed to be such personal torture, John asked:

"Why don't you change jobs?"

"Oh," the younger man replied, "this job pays very well and has lots of security."

He meant financial security, of course, for he certainly felt no personal security, at least while in the air.

"Isn't there anything that helps you when you fly?" John asked him.

"Not really. I've tried both prayer and booze, but neither gives me much comfort. I guess I'm just doomed to tough it out."

My friend is not a person to pry into another's affairs, but he was genuinely concerned about this fellow. He asked yet one more question.

"Do you mind my asking . . . if, when you pray, do you *mean* it or are you just doing an exercise that you feel you ought to go through?"

His companion was thoughtful for a moment, then said, "I guess I've asked myself that same question. What troubles me is that I really don't know. I haven't come up with a satisfactory answer even to myself."

The two sat silently for some time, with the nervous passenger looking out the window, still gripping the seat with all his strength. John was afraid he not only wasn't helping, but that he had actually made the situation worse by asking about his companion's personal faith. But then the young man turned back to him and said:

"Listen, do you pray when you fly?"

"You bet," my friend replied. "But I'll tell you something. I started praying a long time before I started flying. And if there's a difference between your prayer and mine, I guess it must be that I believe in prayer."

John, you see, is one who believes—like me. But, he was a bit unprepared for the young man's next question:

"Why do you believe as you do?"

A simple word . . . *why*. But so often the answer it demands is far from simple. Sometimes we can only stammer as we try to bring our thoughts together— thoughts that are shaded by pent-up emotions and experiences. For most of us, there are no great pillars of polished marble that fit together and rise into a magnificent edifice called "Personal Faith."

On the contrary, personal faith is something that tumbles out of our hearts in spite of ourselves—as we begin to tell the story of our lives. It isn't something cold and isolated, like a temple on a hill—it is a thread woven through the very fabric of our lives. It can't be separated from who we are.

As we start reflecting, the hidden recesses of our mind bring forth those "living parts of our life"—those moments and hours and days when we can trace the distinct and unforgettable touch of the living God.

In my own life, some of those encounters could be likened to "speed bumps"—an abrupt obstacle in my path which compelled me to discover a deeper, more indelible purpose for living.

Just as my friend tried to answer his airplane seatmate, I would like to explore for a moment that haunting "why" question. Why do I believe that God's divine hand has guided my life?

To this point, I have been content in telling you that God *has* provided such guidance. Now I wish to work to a conclusion and share with you how I know what I have been telling you is true.

To do so requires a departure from the approach of the foregoing chapters. Up to now I have been dealing with concrete things, events of my life as they actually happened. What I am suggesting now is that we consider an abstract concept, faith. Faith is somewhat like a dream; it can't be experienced by our senses, but it can be visualized in the mind. Unlike a dream, it can be accepted as fact, something that has actually happened.

Have I convinced you that the events of my life actually happened and were not just an illusion? To this point I think you believe that they occurred as I have explained. (Don't panic, they did.) But *you weren't there.* You have to accept what I have told you—on faith.

If you believe that I have been an honest and reliable source of information, then you can accept what I have told you about myself as being what really happened. In a sense, this is similar to what each of us is faced with when we consider what the Bible has to say about Jesus and His teachings. If we believe in the Bible, then we can accept the validity of His word. And quite simply, if we do believe the Bible and trust what it tells us, then we can know that everything will work out in the best way for those who have faith.

That is not Pollyanna's glad game. It is an unshakable biblical reality.

I can think back on my life and the things that have happened—both "good" and "bad"—that have helped me grow in Christ. Even in adversity I have seen His positive, healing impact on my life. I can say with honesty, assurance, and show by example that there is a Jesus Christ and that a life built around His teachings really works. Believe me, my life proves it!

At each turn of my life, whether I was searching for God's message in times of trouble or praising God for the good fortune that has come my way, I know His hand has guided me. It is His molding that has given direction to my life.

He was there when . . . a child in Augusta was learning to survive with a group of kids that specialized in the "knock-your-block-off" theory of growing up. He gave me courage to overcome a frail body and redirect my athletic ambitions.

He was there when ... a homesick cadet at VPI struggled with thoughts of quitting, giving up, going home. By His strength I was able to benefit from a priceless character-building experience that could never have been duplicated.

He was there when ... a heartsick man in his thirties was rolled into that hospital operating room, with leg wrapped in preparation for cancer surgery. Most certainly, He was there! His tangible presence went with me and comforted me. The parting touch of Marilyn's fingers left me in His firm grasp. Through Him and His grace I was spared.

He was there when ... business success followed business success—when seedling ideas became realities, bearing fruit ten-fold. His guidance provided it, His presence surrounded it, His companionship allowed me to celebrate achievement with a full and thankful heart.

So when adversity came into my life like an ill-behaved shadow of misfortune ... I didn't concentrate on the black cloud, but thought positively about the reality of my God behind it. I admit that I had to do some soul-searching when I had cancer, particularly after living on the point of a pin for five years waiting for the health clearance that would say the disease had been conquered. And yet I have no doubts that God had protected me. *But why*? Why has he spared me and blessed me?

I can sense a direction ... a plan ... a purpose for my life. The truth is He has been hammering constantly at me.

He started with little taps that gave me an appreciation for all the circumstances of living—important and simple, for all types of people—powerful and ordinary, and for all types of adventures—exciting and commonplace.

The worst thing you can do is not make a decision. If a man wants a decision today, give it to him today.

Never say never;
forever is a long
time.

At times the hammer blows have become heavy—painful. It was as if He was saying, "Bob, I am still talking to you, and I want more of your attention."

If you're not offended by the word, I could say that those of us who believe in Christ are the "luckiest" people in the world. Not only are we fortunate in knowing that at death we will have eternal life, but we have the strength and comfort of God's constant presence with us through every moment of everyday living.

I have reason to be especially jubilant because Christ has demonstrated Himself and His power to me again and again throughout my life. He has answered my prayers, not in a subtle way, but in royal fashion. He has done wondrous things. Most of us feel fortunate to have but one "big chance." Mine have been timely and numerous.

This very opportunity to talk directly to you, my friend, is a choice privilege—this chance to demonstrate what belief can accomplish. If this story has offered one thing to you, I hope it is proof that the teachings of Christ can be believed. Christ has been active in my life, and can be in yours, too, if only you have the courage to believe.